CANADIAN REFLECTIONS

Royce
PUBLICATIONS

Text by Rupert O. Matthews
First published in Canada 1984 by Royce Publications.
© 1984 Illustrations and text: Colour Library Books Ltd.,
  Guildford, Surrey, England.
Display and text filmsetting by Acesetters Ltd.,
  Richmond, Surrey, England.
Printed and bound in Barcelona, Spain.
by JISA-RIEUSSET and EUROBINDER.
ISBN 0 86283 196 2

Medicine Lake (above) lies in the mountains of
western Alberta.

The great land of Canada is one of the most beautiful in the world. The infinite variety of the country is beyond comprehension, stretching as it does from beyond the Arctic Circle to the American border and from ocean to ocean. To travel the empty spaces is to enter a magical land where the men and times of yesteryear seem to be captured in the landscape and atmosphere. In the wilderness time seems to slip away and the traveller is lost in a world of dreams.

From Tuktoyaktuk, where white belugas sport in Kugmallit, the long, lonely miles of the Dempster Highway roll away to the south. Driving along the gravel highway the vast treeless tundra that reaches from horizon to horizon and takes hour upon hour to cross emphasises the sheer size of the great northwest. It is almost impossible to believe that Inspector Dempster once made the 640 kilometre journey on nothing more secure than a dog sled. As the moss and lichens give way to forests and mountains one can only wonder at the determination that drove men to brave the savage land in search of wealth.

If the endless ribbon of the dusty northern roads is the only way to travel the great distances, the mountains of the west should be seen on foot. Trails wind between the towering, majestic peaks and past quiet lakes where the only noise is the gentle splashing of leaping trout. During the winter the highlands become freezing hells as the biting winds whip the stinging snow into raging blizzards. But spring brings gentler weather and as the young grass springs underfoot, the mountains seem to echo to the tramp of the mountain men of long ago. The trappers and hunters that pushed forwards the bounds of civilisation made the mountains their own as they walked across the roof of the continent. Today the bushrangers are a different breed, city dwellers that have come to escape the rat-race. But their love of the mountains is no less sincere than that of the hardy men of yesteryear.

On the sweeping plains, where the golden grain stirs in the breeze like the ripples on a lake, the land has been tamed by the plough. But even amongst the barbed wire and tall grain elevators the soughing wind can echo the beat of a thousand hooves and the cries of the cowboys as they drove the herd. Ghosts of long ago.

Among the deep silent woods of the Great Lakes region and the surrounding territory the air is still and the scent of pine needles pervades the air. In the dark interior once roamed the Hurons and Algonquin on their raids into Iroquois territory. As the dry pine needles are stirred by the incautious foot of a moose, it is easy to mistake it for the moccasined tread of an Indian hunter.

The landscapes of Canada affect those who pass through them as no other country on earth. The atmospheric scenery is a jewel that Canadians can see and enjoy just as their ancestors have done for centuries.

(Previous pages, left) Slave River in Wood Buffalo National Park and (previous pages, right) Mount Odaray Plateau in Yoho National Park.

(Above) view to Lobster Cove Lighthouse, Gros Morne National Park and (facing page) Horseshoe Beach in Pukaskwa National Park.

The sweeping prairies have become the richest area of agricultural Canada, (above) in Manitoba and (facing page) in Alberta.

Alberta has greatly varied scenery; (overleaf, left) Athabasca Glacier, Columbia Icefield and (overleaf, right) Astotin Lake.

At extreme ends of the nation are Dickson Falls in
Fundy National Park (above) and Chesterman Beach
in Pacific Rim National Park (facing page).

(Overleaf, left) Big Sky Country in Grasslands
National Park, Saskatchewan and (overleaf, right)
the Peace River in Alberta.

(Above) Hill Island in St. Lawrence Islands National Park and (facing page) Corner Brook, Cape Breton Highlands National Park.

Canada's depleted buffalo herds survive in national parks such as (overleaf, left) Wood Buffalo and (overleaf, right) Waterton Lakes.

The Rocky Mountains hide many lakes, such as
Medicine Lake (facing page) and near Twin Buttes
(above).

(Overleaf) many peaceful stretches of water are
found in Manitoba; (left) Dead Ox Creek and
(right) Clear Lake, Riding Mountain National Park.

New Brunswick remembers its past at Kings Landing
Historical Settlement (facing page). (Above) lobster
traps on the shore of the Gaspé Peninsula, Quebec.

Mount Harkin stands proudly in Alberta (overleaf,
left) and sea mists roll among Sealion Rocks on
the coast of British Columbia (overleaf, right).

Pacific Rim National Park, on Vancouver Island,
includes both Schooner Cove (above) and Long Beach
(facing page).

Gros Morne (above), Newfoundland, has some of the
nation's most dramatic scenery, but Astotin Lake
(facing page), Alberta, has some of the loveliest.

The glow of sunset hangs over Green Point on the
Pacific Coast (above), while smoke fills the air
at Nahanni National Park, Northwest Territories.

Trees shade lakeshores throughout the nation;
(above) Finger Point, Lake Huron, and (facing
page) Maligne Lake, Alberta.

Logs (above) near Stephenville, Newfoundland.
(Facing page) a traditional husky team in the
Northwest Territories.

Astotin Lake (overleaf), in Alberta, changes its
mood with the light.

The roaring waters of Wapta Falls (facing page) in Alberta contrast with the peaceful Ominnik Marsh (above) in Manitoba.

The spreading wheatlands of Manitoba (overleaf) are among the most efficiently farmed areas of North America.

The lakes of Prince Albert National Park, (above)
Amiskowan Lake and (facing page) Waskesiu Lake,
are perhaps its most famous features.

Georgian Bay Islands National Park contains 50 of
the bay's islands, (overleaf, left) Beausoleil
Island and (overleaf, right) Flowerpot Island.

Pukaskwa (these pages) was only created a National Park in 1978 and covers the meeting of the Canadian Shield and Lake Superior.

(Overleaf, left) the borders of Mamalaw Lake in Wood Buffalo National Park and (overleaf, right) marshland in Point Pelee National Park.

Water and rocks are a feature of Canada; (above) in Forillon National Park, New Brunswick and (facing page) on the Maligne River in Alberta.

Boats feature prominently in Canadian life; (overleaf, left) Lake Wapizagonke in Quebec and (overleaf, right) Peggy's Cove, Nova Scotia.

Mount Revelstoke National Park, in British Columbia, contains the Giant Cedars Trail (facing page) and growths of devil's club (above).

(Overleaf, left) tractor in the fertile Okanagan Valley, British Columbia. (Overleaf, right) a seaweed strewn beach in Nova Scotia.

Smoke from a forest fire sweeps the Northwest
Territories near the South Nahanni River (above).
(Right) part of British Columbia's coastline.

(Overleaf) two tranquil stretches of water: (left)
near Heart Lakes in Saskatchewan and (right)
beside Highway 10 in Manitoba.

Much of central Canada is forestland; (facing page) from the Boundary Fire Tower in Prince Albert National Park and (above) in Manitoba.

Elk Island National Park (overleaf), established in 1906, has an area of 195 square kilometres and is thus one of the smallest national parks.

Cold dawn over a tranquil lake in Prince Albert National Park (facing page) and (above) at Lake Kathleen in the Yukon.

The shores of the Great Lakes are among the most scenic in Canada; (overleaf, left) Lake Superior and (overleaf, right) Lake Erie.

(These pages) the autumnal shades that pervade the forests of Quebec, (above) on the shores of Lac à Saur.

The Angel Glacier (overleaf, left) is one of Alberta's finest rivers of ice. (Overleaf, right) a scene from Pacific Rim National Park.

The Inside Passage along the west coast contains some stunning scenery as off Vancouver Island (above) and in Tracy's Arm (facing page).

(Overleaf) trees sprinkle the slopes of the western mountains; (left) Big Beehive, Alberta, and (right) Stanley Peak, British Columbia.